"*Flutter of an Eye*"

Tammy Spears

iUniverse

"FLUTTER OF AN EYE"

iUniverse books may be ordered through booksellers or by contacting:

iUniverse
1663 Liberty Drive
Bloomington, IN 47403
www.iuniverse.com
1-800-Authors (1-800-288-4677)

ISBN: 978-1-5320-3863-1 (sc)
ISBN: 978-1-5320-3864-8 (e)

Print information available on the last page.

iUniverse rev. date: 03/26/2018

Contents

"Flutter of an Eye"

The "Flutter of your Eye" on the day you passed away
Reminds us of a "Butterfly as it gently flies away"
And as we see the grazing deer we know that you are near
We long to hear your voice and see your smile again
And know we will again someday and will hold on to the
memories until then.

We will always remember that day and the
~"Flutter of your Eye" as you drifted away~
Sending our everlasting love and hugs up to you and
We want you to know we are thinking of you!

"Our Mother"

Her heart was so big as the ocean is wide
Her smile was bright as the sun in the sky
We will never forget the last *"flutter of her eye"*

She always thought of others before herself and was loved by everyone who knew her so well

Memories we hold on to keep her near and look forward to the day that we will see her again

Picture taken by Jordan Roberts

"Time"

"Time" moves forward and doesn't go back
So spend your *"Time"* wisely and don't lose track
The *"Time"* you have to spend today
Is *"Time"* you can't get back
It will fade away.

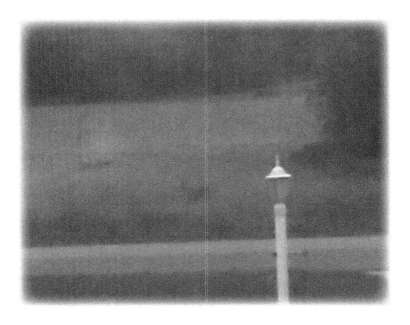

"1st Birthday in Heaven"

When the sun shines from up above
We know it's you sending us your love

If only we could feel your touch for
One more day would mean so much

We think of you every day and hope you know
You are in our hearts and thoughts we pray

Your *"1ˢᵗ birthday in heaven"* is a special one as
You are with the *"Holy One"*

We make a wish that you are at peace and suffer no more
As you rest in the *"House of the Lord"*

3

"One Life"

We only have *"One Life"* in this world to live
God gave it to us as *"our gift to him"*

Cherish each day as it is your last because
As we know they go way too fast

The gift of life God gave to you
To live, to give, to have and share

For He gave it to you on the cross that he bared.

"IMPACT"

I hope the *"Impact"* I had in your life will someday
Bring a smile to your face when I've gone away

The laughter and memories that we hold dear
Will always make you feel that I am near

So make the laughter turn to memories abound and
You will see the *"Impact"* that will surround.

"Your Spirit"

Your touch, your voice, your warm embrace
The bright smile that lights up your beautiful face
These memories of you we hold on to and remember each year
Especially when your birthday is here.
We take comfort in the love that you gave us and
We know *"Your Spirit"* always surrounds us!

Picture taken by Jordan Roberts

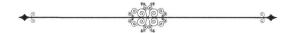

Picture taken by Jordan Roberts

"Precious Time"

Our *"Precious Time"* we do not know
How long on earth we have to go

So use your time as if your last
Enjoy each moment that will become your past

The clock will always tick & tock
It's how in life you walk the walk

On this earth we do not know
How much *"Precious Time"* we have to go

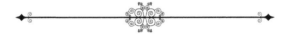

"MOTHER"

Missing you so very much
On our minds today and remembering
The love you gave to all of us
Heaven bound our angel above, we send to you our
Everlasting love
Remembering our *"Mother"* and the memories we made on this special day

Picture taken by Jordan Roberts

The "Walk"

Take my hand and *"Walk"* with me on this journey and enjoy
This gift of life God gave to me
and
All its' Beauty
Share my life and what will be
Take my hand and *"Walk"* with me

"Missing You"

We miss your smile, we miss your face, we miss your love and
Warm Embrace

The years pass on and go so fast but our
memories of you will forever last!

"God's Blessing"

The sweet little child that
"God" sent to you
as A *"Blessing"* from above and his gift to you
To love and to share
With the Family
Is what it's all about as
He *"holds the key"* that fills our hearts with joy

~His gift from above to love forever more~

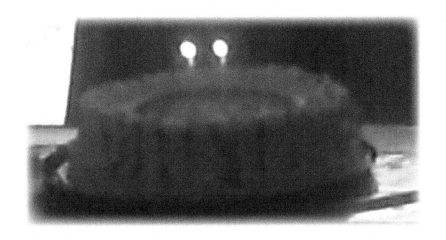

"Year after Year"

Birthdays come and go *"year after year"*
Hold on to each one of them as
They become part of memories past
Make each one count and forever last

As you stare at the candles on the cake
Feeling blessed to have another wish to make

May God grant you another year that
All of your dreams and wishes shall come true

"Year after Year"

The "Sapphire"

As I look at your *"Sapphire"* on my hand
It reminds me of birthdays that we shared
All of the memories we have of you
are
Deep in our hearts
as
We think of you

"Another Day"

Another birthday, another year
"Another Day"
without you here
We miss you very much Mother dear!
We remember our birthdays celebrated together

~Memories of you we hold in our hearts forever~

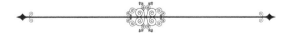

Picture taken by Jordan Roberts

"Salute a Soldier"

"Salute a Soldier" and show your support for
The sacrifices made even lives were cut short
They will always stand tall even after the fall
"Bravery of a Soldier" will be remembered by all!

"Salute a Soldier"
It's the right thing to do
For all that's been given for freedom for you!

The "Void"

The "Void" we feel since you've been gone and
left us here to carry on
We miss your touch and warm embrace and
long to see your smiling face

~The memories we hold dear and miss you still with each passing year~

Picture taken by Tammy Spears

"Memories of my Father-in-Law" (written for my husband)

His laugh was contagious and smile so big
We long to see his face once again

He was a hard worker
he barely made time to rest
The work that he did was done at his best

His kids were his life it was plain to see
The picture of me as I sat on his lap, all the memories of him,
came flooding back

It's been a long time since I've seen his face but
I remember him well like it was yesterday

~I look forward to seeing him again someday~

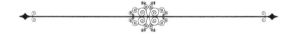

"It's Worthwhile!"

To embrace a child and hug them tight and
See the "joy in their smile" so bright
"It's Worthwhile!"

To hear your better half tell a joke and
Poke fun at you as the brunt of the joke then
"Laughing together" so hard until it brings
Tears to your eyes and you can't see
"It's Worthwhile!"

To hold the hand of a love one as they near
The end of their life
"Giving love and support" as
Their loved one and friend
"It's Worthwhile!"

As we pedal through life
Remember what counts
It's the "little moments" so
Precious and Dear and
All the "love" we left here on earth
"It's Worthwhile!"

Picture taken by Tammy Spears

"Reach for Hope"

"Hope" is something we reach for deep down in our soul
In our time of need when we feel like there is nowhere else to go
"Hope" will always be there in your time of need
Faith, "Hope" and Love three of God's gifts, he gave to you and me

~Always *"Reach for Hope"* in your time of need~

"Time Goes By"

"Time goes by" way too fast as we reminisce about the past
and our memories of you that will forever last
10 years ago you left us here to carry on without you
~Our Beautiful Mother Dear~

The years will fade but not our love for
"Our Angel" watching over us from up above

We will always remember that day and
The *"Flutter of Your Eye"* as you drifted away and
Hold you in our hearts for the love that you gave
And know we will see you again someday.

Sending our everlasting love and hugs up to you
And we want you to know we are thinking of you!

"Another Birthday"

"Another birthday", another year
Another candle on a cake,
Another wish you cannot make
Your loving, giving, caring ways
Are what we miss the rest of our days

We also miss your warm embrace and
That bright smile that lights up your face
We can't believe it's been 10 years and
We wish that you were still here
Our ~Beautiful Mother Dear~

So today we will light a candle in memory of
the birthdays spent with you.
And send our everlasting love and hugs
to our "Angel" up above

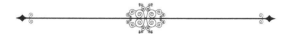

Picture taken by Jordan Roberts

"Autumn Breeze"

The trees so tall and full of leaves
Will become so bare in the *"Autumn Breeze"*
As the color of the leaves swirl in the wind
Reminds us that winter is just around the bin
For now enjoy the colors so bright
That light up the road they cover at night
As the leaves swirl in the *"Autumn Breeze"*
Remember in spring they will again cover the trees

Picture taken by Jordan Roberts

"Christmas Star"

The "Star"

That Shines Bright
Through the Night
That led the way to
Our "Savior and Lord"
That lay in the Manger
We all adore
He will always
Be there for
Your every need
He is our gift at
"Christmas"

You just have to Believe!

Picture taken by Jordan Roberts

"Changed"

How fast the 10 years went by
When we think about them it makes us cry

Our lives have *"Changed"* so much
Since you have gone
and
Left us here to carry on

Our lives have *"Changed"* and will never be the same but
The memories of you we will always hold
Close to our hearts

We want you to know that we love and miss you every day of the year!

Our Step-dad "Pops"

He loved our family as his own
It was obvious in the love that he shown us

He was a book of knowledge no matter the topic
His passion was cars, he was in the business for years
and could fix anything with a vision so clear

He would lend his advice all you would have to do is ask
We all looked up to him as our *dad "pops"* and *"grand-dad"*

He loved our Mother it was plain to see
When he married her he also cared for and loved our family

"Come Together"

Distance sometimes keeps us far apart
even deep within our hearts

But we *"come together"* when in need
that is how it is supposed to be

Through thick and thin
We are always there for our kin

We will always *"come together"* for each other
until the very end

Picture taken by Tammy Spears

"Lend a Hand"

"Lend a hand" to those in need
It could change the life
By showing your love
God's greatest gift from up above

"Lend a hand" and touch the heart
of someone who is looking for a brand new start

"Lend a hand" whenever you can
It is one small part of taking a stand

All by *"Lending a helping hand"*

"The Touch of his Hand"
(written about my husband)

The work that he does on the lawns that he cuts
is done with pride and his *"special touch"*

The care that he shows to each and every one
The traits passed down from his father to his son

He does his best just like he was shown
when his dad was at his side

He does his work with pride with *"the touch of his hand"*
like it was his own

"Take Me With You"

"Take me with you" whatever you do
I will always be a part of you

In the good times, bad times, happy and sad times

"Take me with you" down the road
I will be by your side wherever you go

Part of me lives in you since I've gone away
"Take me with you" I'm there to stay

Picture taken by Tammy Spears

"Life's Blessings"

As I sit back and relax for the night
I reflect upon all the *"blessings"* in my *"life"*

The Lord has been so good to me
The many gifts he has bestowed upon me

A husband, family and friends
I can count on and always depend

Grateful for all he has given to me!

"Furry Friend"
(Our Brooklyn a/k/a Brooksie)

As you come through the door at the end of the day
I wag my tail and kiss your face

I give you a "Whoo" like I'm talking to you
to let you know I love and missed you

I'm excited to play with my frisbee or ball
but most of all
I'm glad you are home now and I won't be alone

Once I am fed and we play a little more
it's off to bed

A new day will start and I will anxiously wait for you to
come through the door to see me again

Picture taken by Tammy Spears

"Morning Sun"

As I tuck myself in for the night
I reflect on the blessings God gave me today

Waiting with anticipation of what the next *"morning"* will bring

and

All of the gifts God has planned for me
Thankful to him for each and every one

Smiling inside at the new *"Morning Sun"*

Picture taken by Jordan Roberts

"Glistening of Snow"

The white *"snow glistening"* outside that you can see far and wide
The ice crystals sparkling in the sun
Like treasured diamonds given to you by a loved one

Fluffy like cotton or cotton candy on a stick
Snow that melts away just as quick

The beauty of the white so innocent and pure
Like an Angel sent down to us on earth from up above

Picture taken by Tammy Spears

"The Touch"

"Touch" a heart in need of love
God's greatest gift from up above

"Touch" a hand in need of holding
The kindness will be felt in the hand you are holding

"Touch" a life of family or a friend
They will remember this when it's time to go

That you *"Touched"* their life by the love you have shown them
God's greatest gift of the three are Faith, Hope and Love he gave to
you and me

"Dream"

"Dream" as big as you want it's never too far
to reach so high and touch the stars

Your *"dream"* could someday lead to some where
you only *"dreamed"* you would be

So reach for your *"dream"* and you will see
it wasn't as far as you thought it would be

"Dream" - "Dream" - "Dream"
Make it a Reality!

Picture taken by Tammy Spears

"The Road of Life"

No one knows in this life how the story will go
As life goes on and we turn each page
In our hearts the story will stay
Even as the years fade away

Every page in the book tells a story of
"The Road" that our *"Life"* took

"Family Bond"
(about our grandparents' family cottage Bangor, MI)

The willow tree we used to climb
The swing we sat on going as high as we could
The neighbors and relatives that gathered around
Whether the picnic table or kitchen table
The fun was had by all

The fish that were caught by grandpa, dad,
uncles and kin every single day
Grandma would clean them with a smile on her face
We would go to the lake for the day
to Swim and jump and play

The fish fries were enjoyed by family and friends
The family, friends and neighbors would stay
and play cards until nights end

Mom would tuck us in to bed before you knew it
up would
pop our heads not wanting the fun to end

The memories were more than fond
It was where as a child we inherited the *"Family Bond"*

The love and laughter that we shared at the cottage
Will forever be in our hearts to stay

"Sisters"

My parents blessed me with two *"Sisters"* to share my love with in life
There for each other through thick and through thin
I couldn't imagine my life without them

The bond that we have is as strong as our faith
We wouldn't have it any other way

As we grow old together through the years
Through happy and sad times, up and down times
Holding hands through laughter and tears

I thank my parents and the Lord above for
My two *"Sisters"* that I adore and love!

"Cherish the Memories"

"Cherish the Memories" of each new day
that you are blessed with along the way

As time fades and you grow old
"Memories" you have stay deep down in your soul
Will be what you look for at the start of each new day

"Cherish the Memories" made along the road
You will realize God gave them to you to have and to hold
As his gift to you as you grow old

Author, Tammy Spears

Picture taken by Jordan Roberts

Printed in the United States
By Bookmasters